CONTENTS

Some words are shown in **bold**, like this. You can find out what they mean by looking in the glossary.

Hunger in Hollywood

On a night in March 2012, a huge crowd gathered outside the Nokia Theatre in Los Angeles, USA. Screaming fans greeted the movie stars Jennifer Lawrence and Josh Hutcherson as they arrived on a special black carpet, rather than the usual red carpet, for a movie **premiere.**

The real star

But the person the crowds wanted to see most was a mother of two from Connecticut, USA, whose imagination had made it all possible. The movie they were so excited about was called *The Hunger Games* and the author's name is Suzanne Collins.

Suzanne Collins arrives at the premiere of *The Hunger Games*, accompanied by her husband.

BREAKING BOUNDARIES

BOX OFFICE HIT

The Hunger Games movie was an instant hit, with worldwide ticket sales of $214.3 million (over £140 million) in its opening weekend. In the United States, the film had the third best opening weekend of all time. It also attracted big audiences in the UK and Australia.

EXTRAORDINARY WOMEN

Suzanne
COLLINS

Nick Hunter

15 238 150 5

Raintree is an imprint of Capstone Global Library Limited, a company incorporated in England and Wales having its registered office at 7 Pilgrim Street, London, EC4V 6LB – Registered company number: 6695582

www.raintreepublishers.co.uk
myorders@raintreepublishers.co.uk

Edited by Nick Huter, James Benefield, and Abby Colich
Designed by Philippa Jenkins
Picture research by Ruth Blair
Production by Helen McCreath
Originated by Capstone Global Library Ltd
Printed and bound in China

ISBN 978 1 406 27397 7 (hardback)
17 16 15 14 13
10 9 8 7 6 5 4 3 2 1

ISBN 978 1 406 27404 2 (paperback)
18 17 16 15 14
10 9 8 7 6 5 4 3 2 1

British Library Cataloguing in Publication Data
A full catalogue record for this book is available from the British Library.

Acknowledgements
We would like to thank the following for permission to reproduce photographs: Alamy pp. 15 (© Photos 12), 19 (© Bernie Pearson); Corbis 16 (© Hero Images), 27 (© Michael Hurcomb), 28 (© Rune Hellestad), 41 (© Rune Hellestad); Getty Images pp. 7 (Larry Burrows//Time Life Pictures), 9 (Popperfoto), 11 (Amy T. Zielinski), 14 (Slaven Vlasic), 18 (The British Library/Robana), 23 (DEA / G. DAGLI ORTI), 25 (Monty Brinton/CBS), 34 (Alberto E. Rodriguez), 35 (FREDERIC J. BROWN/AFP), 43 (Jon Kopaloff/FilmMagic); The Kobal Collection 31 (TOEI), 33 (LIONSGATE); PA Photos pp. 4 (Chris Pizzello/AP), 5 (Victoria Will/AP), 12 (Jennifer Graylock/AP), 22 (Chris Pizzello/AP), 30 (Hubert Boesl/DPA), 36 (Victoria Will/AP), 37 (ABACA), 40 (David Pardo/AP); Photoshot pp. 13 (© TTL), 17, 26 (© STARSTOCK), pp. 29, 32 (© LFI); Scholastic p. 42; Shutterstock pp. 6 (© skyfish), 8 (© Pecold), 10 (© Andrey Bayda), 21 (© Songquan Deng), 24 (© Pavel L Photo and Video), 38 (© shivanetua), 39 (© Jeff Banke).

Cover photograph of Suzanne Collins arriving at the Los Angeles Premiere of *The Hunger Games*, reproduced with the permission of Getty Images (FilmMagic).

In 2010, Suzanne Collins was named as one of the world's most influential people by *Time* magazine.

It was a rare public appearance for the author who usually lets her books do the talking. The huge success of the book **trilogy** and the movies that followed have ensured that Suzanne's name is known around the world. But what is the author's own story? What inspired her to write these dark, but thrilling, books?

True star

Elizabeth Banks, one of the stars of *The Hunger Games*, praised Suzanne at the movie's premiere in 2012:

"For me, the biggest star here is Suzanne Collins who wrote the books. She is the creator of this entire universe and the reason for all this pandemonium."

Growing up

Suzanne Collins was born on 10 August 1962 in Hartford, Connecticut. She is the youngest of four children. Her father was in the US Air Force. When Suzanne was six years old, he left for South East Asia to serve in the Vietnam War. Like many military families, Suzanne's family moved around a lot. They also spent time living in Belgium.

While living in Brussels, Belgium, Suzanne learnt to speak French and some Flemish.

Missing dad

Suzanne admitted that it was hard being the child of a parent in the armed forces:

"If your parent is deployed and you are that young, you spend the whole time wondering where they are and waiting for them to come home. As time passes ... you become more and more concerned – but you don't really have the words to express your concern. There's only this continued absence."

US troops in the Vietnam War were fighting thousands of miles from home.

Coming from a military family would have a big influence on Suzanne and her writing. War was not just something that she saw on television or read about in books. It was very real since her own father, and some of her friends' fathers, went away to fight. Her father suffered nightmares after his experiences.

THEN and NOW

The Vietnam War

Between 1965 and 1973, forces from the United States and other countries fought in Vietnam. They were trying to prevent South Vietnam from being taken over by forces from North Vietnam. More than 2 million people died in the war, including 58,000 Americans. Today, many children of military families have to deal with their parents being absent in distant countries such as Afghanistan.

A writer's education

Suzanne's father also passed his enthusiasm and knowledge of military history on to his children. While they lived in Belgium, they visited lots of ancient castles. The family also learned about Europe's more recent history, including the battlefields that had been fought over during World War I.

Suzanne's father made sure his castle tours did not miss out the gruesome details of medieval warfare.

Living in Belgium

Being in Europe had a big impact on Suzanne. Her father was enthusiastic about military history:

"He would take us frequently to places like battlefields and war monuments ... It was a very comprehensive tour-guide experience. So throughout our lives we basically heard about war."

Being in Belgium also fuelled her love of reading:

"We had next to no television but we had a house full of books."

It was not just Suzanne's experience of war, through her father, that influenced her later in life. Like all writers, reading was very important to her as she developed her own ideas. Suzanne's favourite subject at school was English and she read a lot as a teenager. Her best-loved books include Madeleine L'Engle's *A Wrinkle in Time*. It tells the story of a child's father who has mysteriously disappeared while working on a secret government project. As a teenager, Suzanne liked to read about societies that had gone wrong. Some of her favourite books with this **theme** were George Orwell's *1984* and William Golding's *Lord of the Flies*.

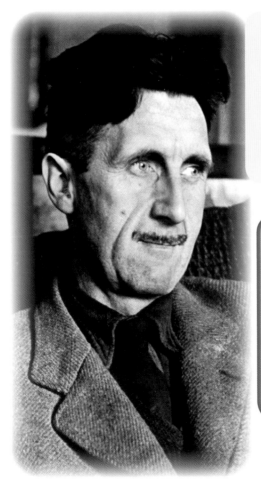

George Orwell's *1984* was **published** in 1949 (but written in 1948). It tells the story of a nightmarish future society. It is easy to see how it may have influenced the Hunger Games trilogy.

Fact:

Suzanne is a fan of old movies that explore war and danger. Her favourites include *The Third Man* and *The Bridge on the River Kwai*.

New York City was a great place for a young writer to learn about writing for theatre and television.

Learning to write

When Suzanne's family returned from living in Europe, they settled in Alabama in the southern United States. Suzanne graduated from the Alabama School of Fine Arts in Birmingham, Alabama, in 1980. Her next move was to Indiana University, where she studied for a qualification in theatre and communication.

The craft of writing

After graduating from Indiana University in 1985, Suzanne's passion for writing took her to New York University, where she completed a masters degree in dramatic writing. Her studies involved writing several plays and **scripts** for theatre, television, and film.

BREAKING BOUNDARIES

A VERY DIFFERENT SKILL

Suzanne's college training was in writing scripts for television. Even as a best-selling author, she still says that she feels like a novice, or a new writer, when writing **prose**.

Suzanne knew that if she wanted to be a writer, it was about more than just having a good idea for a story. She had to learn her craft so the stories and characters she created would capture the interest of her audience.

Suzanne knew she wanted to tell stories on paper or on stage when she enrolled at Indiana University.

Forest Game

While studying at Indiana University, Suzanne appeared in a play called *Forest Game*, in which the college newspaper described the themes as,

> "violent, natural justice of the forest versus the violent, unnatural injustice of the world."

Could this have influenced the Hunger Games trilogy?

11

Personal life

It wasn't just an education that Suzanne gained from her college days. At Indiana University, she met actor Cap Pryor. The couple married in 1992. They lived in New York City from 1987 until 2003, when they decided to move the family out of the city to **rural** Connecticut.

Suzanne has said husband Cap would make a good character for one of her books because he's "good in an emergency".

Living in rural Connecticut is very different from New York City.

Suzanne is also mother to two teenagers, called Charlie and Isabel. Suzanne rarely talks about her family in interviews, and she and her husband have always been very careful to protect the privacy of their family life.

A shy superstar

Journalist Susan Dominus wrote about Suzanne in *The New York Times* on 8 April 2011:

"Collins has always been a **media**-shy figure, given to few public pronouncements ... Collins's readings and appearances are usually off-limits to television cameras, and she declines almost any interaction that involves capturing her on videotape".

BREAKING BOUNDARIES

PRIVATE LIVES

In the world of camera phones and social media, it can seem as if every moment of a **celebrity's** life is in the public eye. Suzanne is not the only author who has tried to keep her personal life and family away from the cameras. J.K. Rowling became one of the world's most famous women because of the success of her Harry Potter series of books, but she has always tried to protect her family from fame.

Writer in demand

When she left college, Suzanne did not sit down and write her first novel. She used her knowledge of **dialogue** and dramatic writing to create scripts for television. Suzanne worked as a writer for Nickelodeon, helping to create series such as *Clarissa Explains It All* and *The Mystery Files of Shelby Woo*.

Clifford the Big Red Dog with his creator, Norman Bridwell.

BREAKING BOUNDARIES

A UNIQUE TALENT

Colleagues could see that Suzanne was different from many TV writers. She was a trained writer and her characters were fully formed like the characters from a book, even if one of them was a drum-playing Kangaroo in *Generation O*.

Suzanne's writing for television was very different from the nightmare worlds she would explore in her later work. *Clarissa Explains It All* was a sitcom for teenagers. Suzanne also worked on shows for younger viewers, such as *Clifford's Puppy Days,* a **spin-off** project from the popular *Clifford the Big Red Dog* series.

Suzanne wrote for several shows for Nickolodeon. Other shows on the channel included *Rugrats*.

One of the shows Suzanne worked on was called *Generation O.* A writer called James Proimos also worked on the show. James Proimos would later have a big impact on Suzanne's career.

THEN and NOW

Television is a route into writing for many authors, but some writers worked in less glamorous or high-profile careers before they got their big break. Master of horror Stephen King worked as a high-school janitor. Charles Dickens started working in a shoe-polish factory at the age of 12. J.K. Rowling taught English to students in Portugal.

How to write for television

Writing for TV is very different from writing novels. When Suzanne is writing a novel, she will come up with every detail of the characters and story. Like all authors, she must create a believable world for those characters. For television writers, that world is often already in place. They are bringing someone else's idea to the screen. Writers will switch from one show to another. However, a fiction author has to stick with their story until it's finished.

THEN and NOW

The growth of children's TV
Before the late 1980s, most children in the United States and elsewhere chose from a small number of channels. The late 1980s saw an explosion in cable TV that created hundreds more channels. This also meant more children's shows, which needed writers.

A team of writers work together to create a television script.

Animators have the task of turning a television writer's words into characters on a screen.

Television writing also involves lots more people. Writers may be part of a team. They also have to listen to many other people, including **directors**, **animators**, and actors. Writing a novel can be a lonely process but television writers have to be prepared to **compromise** with a big team. It is a very talented writer who can master these two very different forms of writing.

Engaging with your readers

In an interview on her publisher's website, Suzanne talks about what it is like to write for different audiences. She says,

> "...whatever age you're writing for, the same rules of **plot**, character, and theme apply. You just set up a world and try to remain true to it."

The Underland Chronicles

Suzanne's friend and colleague James Proimos could see that Suzanne's writing skills and ideas were unique. They could carry her beyond the restricted world of writing for children's television. He persuaded Suzanne to try writing books.

Suzanne was interested in trying something new and she began to think about a story. The character of Gregor and his adventures in the Underland Chronicles started to come together.

THEN and NOW

Wonderland and Underland

The Underland Chronicles were inspired by Lewis Carroll's famous story *Alice's Adventures in Wonderland*, which was first published in 1865. In the story, Alice falls down a rabbit hole and finds herself in Wonderland. Suzanne moved the story to New York City – where there aren't many rabbit holes!

One of the most important parts of a publisher's job is to create a cover design that will stand out.

Getting published

Although she had lots of experience writing for television, Suzanne still had to convince a publisher to take on her books. Publishers do more than simply turn an author's words into a finished book. They also have to sell the book to retailers and others, making sure it is a success. Most fiction books reach a publisher through a literary agent who believes in the author's work. Scholastic published Suzanne's first novel in 2003.

"A gifted writer"

Rosemary Stimola is Suzanne's literary agent:

"I knew from the very first paragraph that she was a gifted writer. From a technical point of view, within very few sentences, she made me care about her main character."

Gregor the Overlander

The first book in the Underland Chronicles told the story of Gregor, an 11-year-old New Yorker. Gregor climbs through a grate in the laundry room of his apartment block and finds himself in the Underland, deep beneath the city's streets. He meets the giant spiders, bats, rats, and cockroaches that live there. Gregor finds himself drawn into the battle for control of the Underland.

Gregor the Overlander was a critical success, which meant it received good reviews. Book industry journal *Publishers' Weekly* said that readers would find Underland "a fantastically engaging place". Readers agreed and the book was a commercial success, which meant it sold many copies. Suzanne went on to create four more books in the series.

Father's advice

While she was writing the Underland Chronicles, Suzanne spent lots of time discussing the story and the battling creatures with her father. She used his military experience to make the battles as realistic as possible. Her father died before the first book was published, but his influence can be seen in much of Suzanne's writing.

BREAKING BOUNDARIES

SERIOUS SUBJECTS

The Underland Chronicles are aimed at children aged under the age of 12. However, Suzanne managed to tackle serious subjects that do not usually feature in many children's books, such as terrorism and war. These subjects would become themes that featured in her later books, too.

In the Underland Chronicles, Suzanne conjured up a world beneath the streets of New York City.

Boy talk

Suzanne writes the story through the eyes of someone completely different from herself. Here, she describes how easy it was to write from the point of view of an 11-year-old boy:

"I remember being 11 very clearly and I had a lot of friends who were boys, so it felt pretty natural being in Gregor's head."

Writer at work

While the stories that spring from Suzanne's imagination are full of excitement, terror, and suspense, the life of a writer has little of this. It is important to be disciplined to write every day. Suzanne has said that she tries to start writing as early as she can in the morning, after a quick breakfast.

Writing takes discipline

Suzanne describes her work habits:

"If I actually write three to five hours that's a productive day. Some days I just stare at the wall. That can be productive, too, if you're working out character and plot problems."

Once a book is written and published, authors have to spend lots of time doing interviews and meeting fans. This helps to sell more books.

THEN and NOW

Ancient storytelling

Many of Suzanne's books are set in the future but her inspiration often comes from the past. Inspiration for the Hunger Games books came from the ancient Greek myth of Theseus and the Minotaur. In the **myth**, the people of Athens are forced to hand over children to be sacrificed. The Hunger Games themselves were inspired by the gladiators of ancient Rome.

In the Greek myth, Theseus kills a beast called the Minotaur and rescues the children of Athens.

Planning

Like most writers, Suzanne plans her work very carefully. She usually divides her books into three sections. Suzanne says this structure comes from her time writing plays that usually had three sections, or acts. Although she plans her books in advance, Suzanne also knows that sometimes things change or new story ideas come up as she is writing.

Fact:
Suzanne loves the life of a writer but if she could do another job, she would want to be an astronomer studying outer space.

War games

One night, Suzanne Collins was lying in bed watching TV. As she flicked through the channels, she saw images of the war in Iraq. She switched channels again and saw a **reality TV** show in which teenagers were competing to win a prize. The two merged in her sleepy brain to form the seed of her next book. At the time, Suzanne could not have predicted the **blockbuster** success of the Hunger Games trilogy.

The gladiators of ancient Rome really did fight to the death to entertain people in arenas like this one.

Selling the idea

The ideas for the story started to come together. Then Suzanne realized that the concept of a young person caught up in war was similar to her previous books. However, the violence and terror faced by the teenage characters of the Hunger Games trilogy was much more real than in the Underland Chronicles.

Suzanne and her agent convinced her publisher that the readers who had enjoyed the adventures of Gregor were now older and ready for the tough future world of the Hunger Games books.

In reality TV shows such as *Survivor*, contestants compete against each other in various tasks and trials. This has parallels with the Hunger Games books.

Hard-hitting subjects

Suzanne has replied to those reviewers who claim that her books are just about growing up:

"I don't write about **adolescence**, I write about war. For adolescents."

Sequels and sales

The Hunger Games was first published in 2008. It was an instant best-seller and fans couldn't wait for the two sequels that completed the trilogy. *Catching Fire* followed in 2009 and the final book, *Mockingjay*, was published in 2010.

By the beginning of 2013, *The Hunger Games* had spent more than 140 weeks on the official US best-seller lists. Almost 10 million copies of the three books had been printed for the US market, and the trilogy was also a huge hit around the world. The e-books also broke records and Suzanne was named the best-selling author on one popular e-reader device.

THEN and NOW

All-time best-sellers

The Hunger Games trilogy still has some way to go before catching up with the best-selling books of all time. For example, J.R.R. Tolkien's Lord of the Rings trilogy (published 1954–1956) has sold an estimated 150 million copies. Book sales are often helped by movie versions, such as the films of the Lord of the Rings trilogy (a still from one of the films is below). However, these films appeared almost 50 years after the books!

Huge displays of books and merchandise in book stores attracted more readers to the trilogy. Of course, the film also attracted more readers to the books too.

Crossover appeal

Like other successful books for young adults (such as the Harry Potter series, and the Twilight books), the trilogy appealed to readers outside the teenage market. Many adults buy these books to read themselves, sometimes in "adult" editions (with a different, more "mature" cover).

Another page-turner

Stephenie Meyer, author of *Twilight* and other books for young adults, reviewed the second instalment of the Hunger Games trilogy, called *Catching Fire*, on her website:

"It's just as exciting as *The Hunger Games*, but even more gut wrenching, because you already know these characters, you've already suffered with them. Suzanne takes the story places I wasn't expecting, and she's never afraid to take it to very hard places ... You won't sleep when you're reading this one."

Kill or be killed

From the very start, the character of Katniss Everdeen dominates the Hunger Games trilogy. Katniss lives in Panem, a nightmarish future version of America ruled by the cruel Capitol. She volunteers to fight in the Hunger Games to protect her sister. Children from across Panem have to battle against each other on live television. The three books tell the story of Katniss overcoming the odds in her rebellion against the Capitol.

Mass appeal

The strong but vulnerable central character of Katniss is a big reason for the success of the books. As well as war and suspense, the books appeal to readers' emotions. Suzanne Collins also explores power and the media, which is fascinating for young readers and adults alike.

BREAKING BOUNDARIES

A TESTING READ

Many reviewers believe that the violence and darkness of the Hunger Games trilogy and in similar books are a new and dangerous trend in young adult books. Critic Meghan Cox Gordon has pointed out that "a careless young reader ... will find himself surrounded by images not of joy or beauty but of damage, brutality and losses of the most horrendous kinds".

The strong character of Katniss is played by the award-winning actress Jennifer Lawrence in the film of *The Hunger Games*.

Balancing act

Best-selling author of children's and young adult fiction Anthony Horowitz also admires the trilogy:

"Suzanne Collins has pulled off a remarkable coup, producing a female character that has equal appeal to both boys and girls and it's interesting how the book manages to balance an intricate and detailed love triangle with sequences of fairly gruesome violence."

The world of the Hunger Games

The most successful stories which appeal to children and young adults create a world of their own. Tolkien created Middle-earth for *The Hobbit* and The Lord of the Rings trilogy, complete with its own myths and languages. The Harry Potter series is set in a magical world. Panem, the world of the Hunger Games books (and films), also feels believable.

Stephenie Meyer's Twilight trilogy and the films it inspired brought her millions of fans.

BREAKING BOUNDARIES

THE YOUNG ADULT BOOM

Authors have always written books aimed at teenagers or young adults. Since the 1990s these books or series have included some of the biggest selling titles of all time, such as the Twilight series of vampire novels. They feature teenage characters but their stories often include serious themes like romance, violence, and horror. Surveys have found that more than half the readers of young adult (or YA) books are actually adults.

In the Hunger Games trilogy, Panem is a **dystopia**. This is a broken society ruled by a dictatorship. The books are set in the future in the area we know as North America. Panem and its brutal government rose up after some kind of environmental disaster. Just as the characters of the books are very real, the world of Panem has been worked out in every detail by Suzanne, even if she doesn't reveal all the details to her readers.

Fact:

The name Panem comes from the Roman phrase *panem et circenses*, meaning bread and circuses. The Roman poet Juvenal said that people would be happy as long as they had food and bloodthirsty games (or circuses).

Some critics have noted similarities between the Hunger Games trilogy and *Battle Royale* (a Japanese book and, then, film). Suzanne has insisted that she had never heard of this before writing the Hunger Games trilogy and has never read the book or seen the film.

Making the movie

With its huge success, it was only a matter of time before the first *Hunger Games* story made it to the big screen. The books' passionate fans guaranteed that any movie would get a lot of attention, and word soon spread through **blogs** and online fan sites.

Keeping control

Many authors have little involvement when their book is filmed. They are not always happy with the results. Suzanne used to write scripts and she wanted to keep control. She wrote a first **draft** of the screenplay for the movie and worked closely with director Gary Ross on everything from the dialogue to casting the actors.

Fact:
Suzanne insisted that the movie should not be made before she had finished the final book, *Mockingjay*. She did not want the way her work was brought to the screen to have an influence on her writing.

Suzanne Collins and Gary Ross have both said how much they enjoyed working together.

THEN and NOW

Special effects

Computer-generated **special effects** (sometimes known as CGI – computer-generated imagery) have made it easier for directors to bring imaginary worlds to life. Special effects were used to create Capitol City and the crowds at the games. In the past, directors would have to build vast stage sets and employ thousands of **extras** to get the same effects.

The novels are narrated by Katniss but the film shows the story from other points of view, such as the control room during the games. Suzanne knew this could be **controversial** with fans.

Book on the big screen

Suzanne wrote a letter to fans on Facebook with her own review of the movie:

"Dear Readers,

I've just had the opportunity to see the finished film of *The Hunger Games*. I'm really happy with how it turned out … The cast, led by the extraordinary Jennifer Lawrence, is absolutely wonderful across the board."

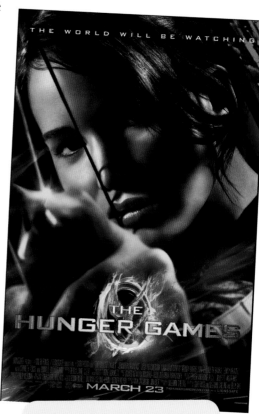

"The world will be watching", promised the poster advertising the movie.

33

Acclaim and awards

The film-makers knew that the books' fans would help to guarantee some success, but the movie's impact surprised everyone. The name Suzanne Collins was familiar to young readers but a Hollywood hit catapulted her to a new level of fame.

The Hunger Games was one of the highest grossing movies of 2012. It was also praised by reviewers. Jennifer Lawrence won the Best Actress category at the MTV Movie Awards and the film won five People's Choice Awards.

Fact:
The Hunger Games' success has inspired new parents when choosing baby names. Rue and Cato have become more popular since the film was released. Katniss and Primrose are both named after types of plant.

The young cast of the movie were praised for bringing Suzanne's characters to life.

Hit movie

Reviewers raved about the film:

"*The Hunger Games* is an essential science fiction film for our times; perhaps the essential **science fiction** film of our times. Whatever your age, it demands to be devoured."

Robbie Collin,
Daily Telegraph

Josh Hutcherson collects an MTV Movie Award for his performance as Peeta.

Everyone's a critic

When a much-loved book is filmed, there are often complaints from the book's fans. The film version may conflict with their own vision of how characters and places look. Some people complained that the skin colour of the actors playing their favourite characters was wrong, although Suzanne said that she was very happy with the choices. There was also criticism from some people about the shaky hand-held camera work.

Who is Suzanne Collins?

While the film attracted huge audiences around the world, the woman at the centre of the amazing story remained hidden from view for the most part. Suzanne has released interviews through her publisher and several are online. But she tries to avoid the spotlight that comes with being one of the world's best-selling authors.

Publicity shy

Some people have suggested that Suzanne is shy. Journalists and others who have met her describe a friendly and approachable person who is just not interested in becoming a celebrity. Like many authors, Suzanne is used to the peace and quiet that she needs to develop strong stories and characters.

A down-to-earth star

Rick Margolis of *School Library Journal* has interviewed Suzanne. Here he offers his thoughts on her personality:

"Suzanne is very, very smart. She's a very deep person and what doesn't really come through in her books is she's also very funny ... You get a real sense that she doesn't take herself too seriously."

In her rare interviews, Suzanne comes across as someone who cares deeply about her characters and how readers respond to them.

With so many media outlets chasing stories, it is hard for anyone in the spotlight to maintain their privacy.

THEN and NOW

Authors and publicity

Suzanne has been described as "reclusive" because she rarely gives interviews. However, the visibility of authors has changed a lot since the days of Jane Austen, one of the greatest English writers. Jane's novels, including *Pride and Prejudice*, were published **anonymously** and their author's identity was not revealed until after her death in 1817. At the time, it was not seen as respectable for women to be authors.

What motivates her?

In an interview in 2011, Suzanne Collins said she had not yet earned much money from her books. Money from book sales can take a long time to reach the author. The success of the Hunger Games trilogy will have now changed her personal fortune, but has wealth changed Suzanne Collins?

Despite her huge success, Suzanne seems to be motivated by the same things that encouraged her to write in the first place. She comes across in interviews as someone who has a passion for books and loves creating stories.

A serious message

Almost all of Suzanne's books have dealt with war. Suzanne is keen for her readers to understand the realities of war. This will lead young people to ask questions about what's going on in the world.

Suzanne's books may be set in imaginary worlds or futures, but the themes she explores are very real.

The world around us

Suzanne hopes her readers think about the issues she raises in her books:

"I want them to ask themselves questions about how elements of the book might be relevant in their own lives, such as: how do you feel about the fact that some people take their next meal for granted when so many other people are starving? What's your relationship to reality TV versus your relationship to the news?"

Suzanne tries to discuss issues in her books. For example, the impact of foreign war on people back home – in her case, in the United States.

Suzanne and her readers

Suzanne is much happier interacting directly with the young readers who buy her books than with the media. She appears at book signings and likes chatting and having her picture taken with fans. The media and video cameras are not allowed.

Suzanne's fans gather outside a movie premiere in London, UK.

Connecting with readers

Suzanne spoke about the letters and other feedback she gets from her readers:

"Some are attracted to the dystopian world, others are there for action and adventure, still others for the romance. The readers are defining the books in very personal and exciting ways."

There are few readers as devoted as the fans of the Hunger Games trilogy. Hundreds of websites are dedicated to it. Books have been written about the world of the Hunger Games trilogy. Fans feel so close to the story that they even criticize choices Suzanne makes about different characters. This was particularly true when *Mockingjay* was published.

Attracting new readers

Suzanne admits to being particularly happy when she hears that someone who does not normally read books is enjoying something she's written. Suzanne has loved reading from a young age and knows the pleasure and success that reading has brought her.

THEN and NOW

Social media

Social media such as Facebook and Twitter mean that authors can have close relationships with millions of readers. Suzanne has avoided this, possibly because she believes that readers should form their own opinions on her books. After all, the Hunger Games trilogy is partly a warning of what can happen when the media goes too far.

41

What's next?

In 2013, the film of *Catching Fire* was released, with *Mockingjay* to follow. If this marks the end of the story for Katniss Everdeen, readers hope that Suzanne Collins will be able to repeat her success with another young adult series.

Year of the Jungle

Suzanne's first book since *Mockingjay* was aimed at a very different audience. *Year of the Jungle* was written for younger children. The inspiration came from Suzanne's own father and the time he spent in Vietnam when she was a child. The main character is a little girl whose father leaves to serve overseas. It is not Suzanne's first book for young children. She wrote a picture book called *When Charlie McButton Lost Power*, which was published in 2005.

Year of the Jungle is illustrated by James Proimos, who persuaded Suzanne to write books in the first place.

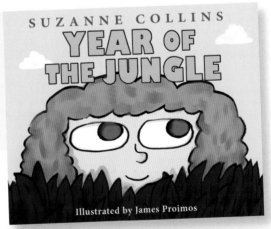

SUZANNE COLLINS
YEAR OF THE JUNGLE
Illustrated by James Proimos

BREAKING BOUNDARIES

BIG QUESTIONS

Suzanne Collins has brought grown-up issues into YA literature. The books are science fiction but the issues of conflict and growing up are faced by millions of people around the world.

Suzanne must be aware people will compare her success with the Hunger Games trilogy with whatever she decides to do next.

Maybe by writing for a younger audience, Suzanne is avoiding trying to repeat the success of the Hunger Games trilogy. Whether she matches that success or not, Suzanne Collins's stories will continue to fascinate readers for many years to come.

Looking to the future

Suzanne spoke to the *Observer* newspaper about her future as a writer:

"I'm not a very fancy person. I've been a writer a long time, and right now *The Hunger Games* is getting a lot of focus. It'll pass. The focus will be on something else. It'll shift. It always does. And that seems just fine."

Glossary

adolescence teenage years, during which we all change from being a child to an adult

animator artist who works on animated films or cartoons

anonymous person whose name is unknown, or who has chosen not to reveal their name

blockbuster film or book that is hugely successful

blog short for weblog, an online journal on any topic

celebrity person who is well known

compromise when a person is prepared to give up something they want in order to reach an agreement with someone else

controversial something that stirs up a public debate because people have conflicting opinions about it

dialogue conversation between characters in a book, play, or film

director person in charge of making a film or staging a play

draft early attempt to write something. There may be several drafts before a book or film script is completed.

dystopia imagined nightmare society where something has gone very wrong

extra person who has a very small role in a film, such as part of a crowd scene

media name for all means of communication, such as television, radio, newspapers, and online information

myth traditional story that often involves magic or monsters. The ancient Greeks created many myths.

plot what happens in a story

premiere first showing of a film or play, which usually features appearances from its actors and other celebrities to draw attention to the film

prose ordinary writing that is organized in paragraphs, rather than poetry or a play script

publish make information or ideas available to many people, such as in a printed book or on the web

reality TV programmes that feature ordinary members of the public, which can include talent shows or documentaries about their lives

rural describes something in the countryside

science fiction stories set in an imagined world that has been changed by science or technology

script document that includes words spoken by actors and stage directions used in making a film, play, or television programme

special effects visual effects created for films, often using computers to show something that could not actually be filmed

spin-off TV series, book, or film that focuses on a minor or supporting character from another TV series, book, or film. A minor character is now the main character in this story, so we learn more about his or her life.

theme subject or topic that is used frequently in a work of art or in a collection of works from a particular artist or period

trilogy collection of three books or films that tell an overall story

Timeline

1962   Suzanne Collins is born in Hartford, Connecticut, USA, on 10 August

1980   Suzanne graduates from the Alabama School of Fine Arts in Birmingham, Alabama

1985   Suzanne is awarded a degree in communications and theatre studies from Indiana University

1991   Suzanne begins work as a writer for children's television

1992   Suzanne marries actor Cap Pryor, who she met at college

2003   *Gregor the Overlander*, the first title in the Underland Chronicles, is published, followed by four more books in the series between 2003 and 2007

2005   Suzanne writes a picture book for younger readers called *When Charlie McButton Lost Power*

2008   Publication of *The Hunger Games*

2010   Suzanne Collins is named as one of the world's most influential people in *Time* magazine

        Publication of *Mockingjay*, the final book in the Hunger Games trilogy

2012   *The Hunger Games* movie opens. It is one of the most successful first weekends of all time.

2013   Suzanne Collins publishes *Year of the Jungle*, a book for younger children illustrated by James Proimos

Find out more

Books
Suzanne Collins (Remarkable Writers), Megan Kopp (Weigl Publications, 2012)

Suzanne Collins: Words on Fire (USA Today Lifeline Biographies), Marcia Amidon Leusted (21st Century Books, 2012)

The World of the Hunger Games, Kate Egan (Scholastic, 2012)

Writers (21st Century Lives), Debbie Foy (Franklin Watts, 2010)

As well as reading Suzanne's books, you can also seek out some of the books that influenced her writing, such as George Orwell's *1984*.

Websites
www.bbc.co.uk/programmes/b01d84g5
BBC Radio produced a profile of Suzanne Collins in 2012. You can listen to it here.

www.scholastic.com/thehungergames/media/suzanne_collins_q_and_a.pdf
The website of Suzanne's publisher includes an extended interview with the author.

www.suzannecollinsbooks.com
This is Suzanne's official website, which includes interesting details of her life and work.

Further research
Here are a few topics you could investigate:
- One of the most difficult parts of being an author is getting your book published in the first place. Investigate how your favourite authors got published.
- Find out more about Suzanne Collins's influences, from Greek myths to the books she loved as a child.
- What's the latest news on Suzanne Collins? What is she planning to write next and when will it be coming out?

Index